YOUR KNOWLEDGE HAS VALUE

- We will publish your bachelor's and master's thesis, essays and papers

- Your own eBook and book - sold worldwide in all relevant shops

- Earn money with each sale

Upload your text at www.GRIN.com and publish for free

Bibliographic information published by the German National Library:

The German National Library lists this publication in the National Bibliography; detailed bibliographic data are available on the Internet at http://dnb.dnb.de .

This book is copyright material and must not be copied, reproduced, transferred, distributed, leased, licensed or publicly performed or used in any way except as specifically permitted in writing by the publishers, as allowed under the terms and conditions under which it was purchased or as strictly permitted by applicable copyright law. Any unauthorized distribution or use of this text may be a direct infringement of the author s and publisher s rights and those responsible may be liable in law accordingly.

Imprint:

Copyright © 2018 GRIN Verlag
Print and binding: Books on Demand GmbH, Norderstedt Germany
ISBN: 9783668718449

This book at GRIN:

https://www.grin.com/document/418703

Carl Robert Giersch

How can we write Graeco-Roman history from the point of view of the poor?

GRIN Verlag

GRIN - Your knowledge has value

Since its foundation in 1998, GRIN has specialized in publishing academic texts by students, college teachers and other academics as e-book and printed book. The website www.grin.com is an ideal platform for presenting term papers, final papers, scientific essays, dissertations and specialist books.

Visit us on the internet:

http://www.grin.com/

http://www.facebook.com/grincom

http://www.twitter.com/grin_com

How can we write Graeco-Roman history from the point of view of the poor?

The history of Graeco-Roman societies is a history of division and class struggle. Every city, every country and every empire has always been divided between the plebeians and the patricians, between the aristocrats and the peasants: between the rich and the poor. However, if we speak about antiquity, we consider almost exclusively the upper-class perspective, the perspective of the wealthy and of the nobles – even though the majority of the world was poor or enslaved. This essay aims to prove that we can see Graeco-Roman History from the point of view of the poor only as the view of a whole class. Although it does not discuss the problem of slavery, only the issue of poor, unfree and otherwise fettered peoples. Exploring primary and secondary accounts: two Greek authors, the theory of Marx and the arguments of de Ste. Croix will demonstrate that we are only able to see their point of view of the poor based on generalisation, always with another aim than writing the history from the point of view of the poor. We can only explain societal movements but cannot explore personal and individual motivations.

Solon, a statesman who discussed political matters in his poetry, states in one of his remaining accounts: "ἴσόν τοι πλουτέουσιν, ὅτῳ πολὺς ἄργυρός ἐστι καὶ χρυσὸς καὶ γῆς πυροφόρου πεδία ἵπποι θ' ἡμίονοί τε, καὶ ᾧ μόνα ταῦτα πάρεστι, γαστρί τε καὶ πλευραῖς καὶ ποσὶν ἁβρὰ παθεῖν." He discusses society here in terms of a strong contrast. On one side the poor, on the other side the rich. This demonstrates the dependence of social status on material ability yet argues that social position should be independent of material and financial status. A second fragment says: "πολλοὶ γὰρ πλουτεῦσι κακοί, ἀγαθοὶ δὲ πένονται." This reveals the general Ancient cliché of 'the richer the person, the better' and clearly states the ability of poor people to behave like the ideal rich person. Solon gives through his poems valuable information and outlines the situation of the poor quite clearly. It describes their awareness of being on the lowest level of the social hierarchy and mirrors the poor people's opinions on being both subordinate labourers and equal members of the state and democracy. Moreover, it gives an overview of their general situation: the poor did not possess any material goods and were without any financial insurance; standing in need of both of them. Solon aims to give a very objective view on

Athens' poor and their problems. However, he relies too much on general assumption and contrasts both classes to an exaggerated extreme. Hence, Solon´s view of poverty (of those who are free citizens, not those who are enslaved or working as unfree labourers) is "not one from experience, but one from an outsider looking in," as a contemporary scholar states. Even though Solon was born into a wealthy family, he apparently cared about the poor. In the 6th century BC, he reformed the Athenian democracy.

Solon, a statesman who discussed political matters in his poetry, states in one of his remaining accounts: "ἰσόν τοι πλουτέουσιν, ὅτῳ πολὺς ἄργυρός ἐστι καὶ χρυσὸς καὶ γῆς πυροφόρου πεδία ἵπποι θ' ἡμίονοί τε, καὶ ᾧ μόνα ταῦτα πάρεστι, γαστρί τε καὶ πλευραῖς καὶ ποσὶν ἁβρὰ παθεῖν."[1] He discusses the society here in strong contrast. On one side the poor, on the other side the rich. It displays the social status´ dependence on material ability yet argues that the social position should be independent of material and financial status. A second fragment says: "πολλοὶ γὰρ πλουτεῦσι κακοί, ἀγαθοὶ δὲ πένονται."[2] Thereby, it reveals the general Ancient cliché of 'the richer the person, the better' and clearly states the ability of poor people to behave like the ideal rich person. Solon gives through his poems valuable information and outlines the situation of the poor quite clearly. It describes their awareness being on the lowest level of the social hierarchy and mirrors the poor people´s opinion, namely not only being subordinate labourers yet equal members of the state and democracy. Moreover, it gives an overview of their general situation: the poor did not possess any material goods, were without any financial insurance; standing in need of both of them. Solon aims to give a very objective view on Athens' poor and their problems, however, he relies too much on general assumptions and contrasts both classes to an exaggerated extremum. Hence, Solon´s view of poverty (of those who are free citizens, not those who are enslaved or working as unfree labourers) is "not one from experience, but one from an outsider looking in,"[3] as a contemporary scholar states. Even though Solon was born

---

[1] Gerber, D. E. 1999. *Greek Elegiac Poetry: From the Seventh to the Fifth Centuries BC*. Harvard: Fragment 14
[2] Ibid. Fragment 24
[3] Ryan, V. 2015. *Poverty Trancending Time: A Case Study of Four Ancient Greek and Latin Texts Discussing Poverty*. Indiana: p. 6.

into a wealthy family, apparently cared about the poor. In the 6th century BC, he reformed the Athenian democracy.

Aristophanes, a playwright discussing social issues in a comic manner, argues in his play "Πλοῦτος" through the character of the farmer Chremlyos: "(ὅ τι) τοὺς χρηστοὺς τῶν ἀνθρώπων εὖ πράττειν ἐστὶ δίκαιον, τοὺς δὲ πονηροὺς καὶ τοὺς ἀθέους τούτων τἀναντία δήπου… ἢν γὰρ ὁ Πλοῦτος νυνὶ βλέψῃ καὶ μὴ τυφλὸς ὢν περινοστῇ"[4] He describes wealth as somewhat positive which should be given to the good men, meaning independent from social status. Antithetical, the bad (those who are godless and wicked) shall not reach this wealth. The second part of the quote displays the progress that has been done. The protagonist of Aristophanes' comedy gives in the further lines an explanation of the discussed wealth and poverty: "οὔκουν εἶναί φημ', εἰ παύσει ταύτην βλέψας ποθ' ὁ Πλοῦτος, ὁδὸν ἥντιν' ἰὼν τοῖς ἀνθρώποις ἀγάθ' ἂν μείζω πορίσειεν."[5] Both wealth and poverty, are personified and hence of equal importance. Aristophanes stages the poverty (meaning here the poverty under free citizen, not the poverty of slaves or unfree labourers) as something bad which has to be vanquished, so he and the Athenian society must have been highly aware of its problematic nature. Aristophanes introduces the wealth as something which isn't entirely material and financial – for him, it is partly based on human interaction, i.e. honour. By choosing the two farmers Chremlyos and Blepsidemos as protagonists, the author of this play clearly attempts to give a subjective insight to the daily life of the lower class, which stands complementary to the objective and reflective chorus of the play. Thereby, displaying and discussing current matters and issues, he makes it a "somewhat moralizing work"[6] as a 21st-century scholar states, however, his satire also attacks and questions moral itself. Aristophanes is most-likely influenced by his contemporary Socrates' approaches which include the questions what person one should be and what person one can be. As he lived during Athens' most radical form of democracy, he didn't only experience citizenship without a dependence on the status of birth and

---

[4] https://www.loebclassics.com/view/aristophanes-wealth/2002/pb_LCL180.417.xml; accessed 22/01/2018, 2.14 pm (Online Version of: Aristophanes. 2002. *Frogs. Assemblywomen. Wealth.* Harvard: Jeffrey Henderson.)
[5] Ibid.; accessed 22/01/2018, 2.36 pm
[6] https://www.britannica.com/biography/Aristophanes#ref404922; accessed 21/01/2018, 4.30 pm

property, but also its downside: the extreme form of poverty, one's inability to feed oneself occurred under the free lower-class citizens.

To conclude the essay's first section: Solon and Aristophanes are both aiming to show the poverty's role in society in its entirety and only the latter one in its specifics. Trying to give an objective overview, Solon refers too often to generalisations as that we could consider him as a reliable source for an insight into the poor's perspective. Per contra, Aristophanes is able to give not only a subjective perspective but also an objective reflection. Therefore, we can write history from the point of view of the free poor in different ways: we can describe their daily lives, their situation and their role and position in society, when comparing and combing different primary sources, backed up with detailed evidence. However, both don't discuss the role and life of slaves and the unfree poor, therefore we can't – and this is valid for the main 'daily-life' primary accounts – access the slaves' and unfree labourer's situation. Overall, the topic is not discussed as a matter of fact, but as a matter of the big picture – here the Athenian society. Furthermore, it must be discussed whether secondary sources, discussing a wide range of primary sources and other ancient and modern historians, analysing the Graeco-Roman history, are able to write history from the poor's perspective.

This paragraph will discuss one of the major works of de Ste. Croix who gives, as he states it, a "Marxist interpretation of Greek history"[7], he is very concerned about all social issues and discusses them very well. The author does not only describe and explain Marx's class theory in relation to the Ancient history in such detail as no one did before but also aims to describe the slave's daily lives and needs. He completely follows Marx by displaying the class struggle of the antiquity as a struggle between the rich masters and their poor slaves. In his third chapter, for instance, he lists the main characteristics and problems: a higher mortality than the middle-class, higher percentage of women, more pregnancies and therefore more children.[8] Being a Marxist, he only passionately emphasises with the Slaves and reveals a picture of their daily lives to prove Marx's class theory, not because he's

---

[7] De Ste. Croix, G. 1981. *The Class Struggle in the Ancient Greek World.* London: p. 30
[8] Ibid.: p. 229-231

naturally concerned about their being. He explains the "gradual change in the forms of exploitation"[9] through the upper-class slaveholders. De Ste. Croix, therefore, uses the situation of the poor just to explain their role and function in Marx's system. He doesn't mention the views of Finley, Weber and Welskopf regarding the important points: and if he discusses them then only to attack them in a polemic manner, proving and defending Marx's argument. Consequently, the author doesn't mention personal and private views and only uses the discomfort and problems of the slaves to prove the big picture: that the society is an opposition between master and slave. He gives here an objective account insofar as he doesn't try to write history from the point of the view, however, wants to display the poor's situation from an outsider's view.

Nevertheless, even if de Ste. Croix attempts to display the situation of the poor, his definition of poverty and his view of the situation in the Ancient Greek world are extraordinary and differ heavily from contemporary – and certainly Neo-Marxist perspectives. Unlike Weber, coming from a universal-historical perspective, therefore seeing modern capitalism as unique, he argues completely like Marx: explaining the Graeco-Roman history as part of an ongoing process. That progress is essentially the process of the Capitalism, its end and a following socialism and communism. However, it is still unclear what the poor are after de Ste. Croix's definition.

He defines the poor only as the class of the enslaved unfree beings – so just slaves and serfs. He doesn't consider the role and situation of the free poor. His argument throughout the chapter III is that the slaves were more important for the economy and that there generally was a higher percentage of unfree inhabitants than free citizens.[10] However, modern investigation falsified his proposition completely: the percentage of unfree people was low, therefore the serfs and slaves had actually a small importance for the Ancient Greek economy. Moreover, he doesn't mention the metics at all. Even though, de Ste. Croix could have been aware of these facts, he even exaggerates the importance of the slaves, stressing "the ideological effects of slavery over its economic function"[11] as a

---

[9] Ibid.: p. 230
[10] Ibid.: p. 226-259
[11] Golden, M. 1984. *A Marxist Classic*. Labour/Le Travail, 14, p. 212.

contemporary scholar states. He explains social relationships between the class of the unfree to the class of the rich and ruling citizens. De Ste. Croix states two possible approaches regarding the interlinking of the classes. The relation between the ruling class and the serving free citizens and – for him way more important – the relationship between the master and his slave. [12] He discusses and describes the latter one over several pages, per contra, he never comes back to the relationship between the classes of free inhabitants.[13] Even though, Weber discusses this topic as the more realistic and essentially more important. This proves once again his stubborn manner, only referring to the enslaved inhabitants as the poor.

Overall, Dr. de Ste. Croix focusses only on an analysis, description and explanation of the historical foundation for Marx´s proposal. Albeit, he gives a quite detailed description of the poor´s situation[14] and especially their relation to other classes of the social hierarchy, his understanding of what the poor are is very uncommon. Therefore, he only considers a minority of the poor and the entirety of those who had to face poverty.

Summa Summarum, there have been various attempts to write Graeco-Roman history from the point of view of the poor: Solon´s and Aristophanes exploration of the ancient society and Marx´s and de Ste. Croix´s argumentation and explanation of the past. We can only see Graeco-Roman history through the lenses of generalisations, being part of a bigger picture – and that is valid from the Proto-Marxist Aristoteles until Finley). There will never be a better or a worse perspective on their lives – in this case, an extreme subjectivity of primary sources would be extremely helpful. Essentially, we will never be able to describe personal and private perspectives, aims and views, however, we can access their role in the society and thereby explore their daily lives.

---

[12] Ibid.: p. 206
[13] Ibid.: p. 205-275
[14] Ibid.: p. 231

YOUR KNOWLEDGE HAS VALUE

- We will publish your bachelor's and master's thesis, essays and papers

- Your own eBook and book - sold worldwide in all relevant shops

- Earn money with each sale

Upload your text at www.GRIN.com
and publish for free